Waking Up My Purpose

A Journey of Faith, Healing, and Truth

Tequeya L. Spann

Tequeya L. Spann

Waking Up My Purpose

ISBN: 979-8-9951821-0-8

For permission requests, contact:

Walking With a Purpose, Gary, Indiana

www.wwpurpose.com

Tequeya L. Spann

To:

____

Contents

Dedication

"I can do all things through Christ which strengtheneth me." — Philippians 4:13 (KJV)

This book is dedicated to every woman who has ever felt lost, unseen, or unworthy.

To those who have cried in silence, prayed for peace, and longed for purpose, know that your story matters.

To every mother, daughter, sister, and friend walking through storms—this book is for you.

May you find hope in your healing, strength in your surrender, and joy in rediscovering who you are in Christ.

And to God, my Father and my strength, thank You for never letting go, for turning my pain into purpose, and for giving me the courage to write this book.

Family Dedication

Before anything else, I want to give all glory and honor to God.

Thank You, Lord, for choosing me, for keeping me, and for using me as a vessel to speak Your truth. Thank You for Your grace, Your mercy, and Your strength. Every word in this book exists because of You. I am nothing without Your guidance, and everything I do, I do to glorify Your name.

I also want to thank my Pastor, whose leadership, prayers, and spiritual covering have helped guide me through many seasons of growth. Thank you for pouring into me, encouraging me, and reminding me of who I am in Christ.

This book is lovingly dedicated to my six children, my beautiful grandchildren, and to every child I've cared for through my childcare and the ones I've adopted in love.

You are my heart, my inspiration, and my purpose. Every lesson, every moment, every challenge has shaped me into the woman God created me to be.

To my mother, **Jacquelyn Davis**, thank you for standing by me with strength, faith, and unconditional love. Your support has carried me through the darkest storms and the brightest victories. I am forever grateful for the foundation you built within me.

And to every friend and family member who has encouraged, supported, loved, and uplifted me—thank you. Your prayers, your kindness, and your belief in me helped me keep going even when the journey felt heavy.

May God bless each of you for the love you have given.

Tequeya L. Spann

CHAPTER 1

Faith: Walking in What You Cannot See

"Now faith is the substance of things hoped for, the evidence of things not seen."
Hebrews 11:1 (KJV)

Faith is more than a word; it is the quiet strength that moves us when we cannot see the outcome.

There were times when I tried to walk by sight, when I wanted proof before I believed, but the Lord reminded me that faith doesn't wait for clarity; it acts in trust.

There are moments when life feels uncertain, when it seems as if God is silent and the world is loud. But faith whispers, "Hold on." It reminds us that storms are temporary and that the same God who calmed the sea still commands peace over our lives today.

True faith grows not in comfort, but in challenge. It's easy to praise when everything looks right, but faith is tested when you don't understand the "why." In those moments I learned that God's silence isn't His absence—it's His invitation to trust.

Faith changes how we see ourselves. When you know that God's hand is on your life, you stop trying to prove your worth to others. You no longer measure your success by worldly standards; instead, you rest in knowing that obedience brings blessings in due time.

A Moment of Reflection

• Think of a time when God asked you to move before you saw the result.

• How did your faith grow from that experience? What did you learn about yourself and about God's timing?

Closing Prayer

Heavenly Father, strengthen my faith when I cannot see. Help me to trust Your hand even when I can't understand Your plan. Let my heart rest in knowing that You are working all things for my good. Teach me to walk in boldness, not by sight but by faith.

Amen.

Summary Notes...

CHAPTER 2

Relationships: Knowing Your Worth

"Above all else, guard your heart, for everything you do flows from it."
Proverbs 4:23 (KJV)

Relationships have a way of revealing who we are our strengths, our wounds, and our growth. For a long time, I looked for someone to complete me, not realizing that God had already made me whole.

When we forget our worth, we often accept less than we deserve. We try to heal what's broken in others, while ignoring the cracks within ourselves.

I learned that love should never cost you your peace. True love is built on respect and patience, and grace. When you know who you are in Christ, you stop chasing validation from people who can't see your value.

It's easy to mistake attention for affection and possession for partnership. But attention fades, and manipulation masquerades as care.

Real love lifts you closer to God—it doesn't pull you away. If a relationship makes you hide who you are, it's not love, it's control.

There are still good men and good women in this world. But we must first become who we seek.

When you carry yourself with dignity and compassion, the right people will recognize your light without you having to dim it.

A Moment of Reflection

• What patterns have you noticed in your past relationships?

• What can you do differently to invite peace and godly love into your life?

Closing Prayer

Lord, teach me to love without losing myself. Help me to wait for what is true and honorable in Your sight. Remove from me the desire to settle for what does not serve my soul. Let every relationship I enter reflect Your heart and Your purpose.

Amen.

Summary Notes...

CHAPTER 3

Self-Respect: Becoming Whole in Christ

"I will praise Thee; for I am fearfully and wonderfully made: marvelous are Thy works; and that my soul knoweth right well."
Psalm 139:14 (KJV)

Self-respect begins when you understand that you are made in the image of God. You are not an afterthought; you are chosen, loved, and designed with intention.

When you forget that truth, the world will try to define you by its standards, your looks, your money, your relationship status. But God defines you by purpose, not popularity.

I used to think I needed approval from people to feel worthy. Then I learned that when you live for the applause of others, you lose your own peace.

Respecting yourself means setting boundaries and knowing when to say "no" without guilt. It's realizing that your time, energy, and spirit are sacred.

When you walk with God, your confidence shifts. You stop begging people to see your value, because you know your worth isn't up for debate.

A Moment of Reflection

- Do I treat myself the way I want others to treat me?

- Have I allowed anyone to make me forget my worth?

- How can I show respect for myself in the way I speak, act, and live?

Closing Prayer

Lord, help me see myself the way You see me. Remind me that I am fearfully and wonderfully made. Teach me to walk in dignity and grace, to love myself without pride, and to honor You with every choice I make.

Amen.

Summary Notes...

CHAPTER 4

Parenting: Guiding with Grace and Purpose

"Train up a child in the way he should go: and when he is old, he will not depart from it." — Proverbs 22:6 (KJV)

Parenting is one of the greatest responsibilities and blessings that God could ever give us. It's not just about raising children; it's about shaping hearts, molding character, and teaching them the ways of the Lord.

Our children don't always do what we say, they do what they see. If we want them to walk in love, we must show them love. If we want them to respect others, we must live a life of respect for ourselves.

It's not about being perfect; it's about being present, patient, and prayerful.

A Moment of Reflection

• Am I showing my children the same grace I ask God to show me?

• Do my actions teach them faith, forgiveness, and love?

• How can I make prayer part of our daily life together?

Closing Prayer

Heavenly Father, thank You for trusting me with the gift of parenthood. Give me the wisdom to lead with love, the patience to teach with kindness, and the faith to know that even when I fall short, You are still in control. Let my children see Your light through me and grow to walk boldly in their purpose.

Amen.

Summary Notes...

CHAPTER 5

Purpose: Walking Boldly in God's Plan

"For I know the thoughts that I think toward you, saith the Lord, thoughts of peace, and not of evil, to give you an expected end."
Jeremiah 29:11 (KJV)

There comes a time when you must stop running from who God called you to be. For so long, I was searching for some kind of peace, identity, direction but I realized what I was looking for was already inside of me.

God had planted purpose within me before I even took my first breath. Walking in purpose doesn't mean life will be easy; it means you've decided to trust God even when it's hard.

It's understanding that your pain, your past, and even your mistakes are part of a bigger picture. Nothing you've gone through is wasted.

Every tear, every trial, every setback is shaping your story.

A Moment of Reflection

• What has God placed on your heart that you've been afraid to pursue?

• What excuses have kept you from walking in your calling?

• Are you ready to trust God's plan, even when you don't understand it?

Closing Prayer

Lord, reveal to me the purpose You've placed within my heart. Give me courage to walk boldly in faith and to surrender my fears to You. Remind me that my purpose is not about me—it's about bringing glory to Your name. Use my story to uplift others and to show the world that You are faithful.

Amen.

Summary Notes...

CHAPTER 6

Healing: Letting Go, Trusting God, and Moving Forward

"He healeth the broken in heart, and bindeth up their wounds."
Psalm 147:3 (KJV)

Healing is not something that happens overnight; it happens when you allow God to work on the places in your life you don't talk about. Many people want healing, but they don't always want to feel or face the truth behind the pain.

Healing takes faith. Faith to believe that God can fix what feels shattered. Faith to trust that the pain you survived won't define your future. Faith to let God close doors you would've kept open out of comfort or fear.

Healing also requires forgiveness, even when it hurts. Not for them, but for you. Forgiveness doesn't make what happened "okay." But it frees your heart so God can heal it.

If you want true healing, you must check your heart:

- Am I holding onto anger?

- Do I still replay painful moments in my mind?

- Am I carrying bitterness that blocks my blessing?

- Have I forgiven the person but still rehearsed the memory?

God can't heal what you pretend doesn't hurt. Healing requires telling God the truth: "Lord, this still bothers me. I need You." You have to make a decision to release what broke you so you can receive what God has for you. Holding onto old wounds keeps you stuck in old seasons.

And when God starts healing you, don't go back to what wounded you. Don't open doors God shut. Don't return to old habits, old cycles, or old emotions. Don't revisit what God rescued you from.

If you believe God can heal you — stand on it. Don't keep doubting your own breakthrough. Don't second-guess your growth. Don't let fear make you return to the place God delivered you from.

Healing is a process, but wholeness is the promise.

A Moment of Reflection

• Who or what do I need to release to fully heal?

• Have I forgiven myself for the mistakes I've made?

• Am I holding onto anything that God told me to let go?

• How can I invite God deeper into my healing process today?

Closing Prayer

Lord, I surrender every hidden wound to You. Heal the parts of me I don't show to anyone. Help me forgive myself and others. Remove every offense, bitterness, and emotional weight from my heart. Strengthen my faith to believe in the healing I cannot yet see. Teach me to move forward with grace, wisdom, and peace. Remind me that my story is not over, it is just beginning.

Amen.

Summary Notes...

Tequeya L. Spann

CHAPTER 7

Truth: Recognizing the Enemy's Schemes

"Be sober, be vigilant; because your adversary the devil, as a roaring lion, walketh about, seeking whom he may devour."
1 Peter 5:8 (KJV)

There is a spiritual battle happening all around us—one that we can't always see but can surely feel. The enemy's greatest weapon isn't always destruction; it's deception. He wants us distracted, discouraged, and disconnected from God.

I used to think that if life was hard, God had left me. But I learned that the struggle isn't a sign of abandonment—it's proof of purpose. The enemy doesn't fight what isn't a threat. When he sees potential, he tries to plant confusion.

That's why we must stay rooted in truth. You

have to be careful what voices you allow in your ear. Everyone speaking to you isn't speaking for you. Some words are meant to build; others are meant to break. That's why prayer and discernment are your greatest defenses. When you know God's Word, you can recognize the enemy's lies. We can't defeat what we won't confront.

The devil wants to convince you that you'll never be enough, that you're too damaged to be used by God—but that's a lie straight from hell. God uses broken people to build beautiful testimonies.

Every time you pray, every time you choose peace over anger, love over hate, forgiveness over revenge, you are winning spiritual battles that the world can't see. Don't underestimate the power of your obedience. The enemy trembles when you stand on truth.

A Moment of Reflection

- Have I been listening to the wrong voices in

my life?

- What thoughts or habits keep me bound that I need to surrender to God?

- How can I strengthen my spirit to resist the enemy's lies?

Closing Prayer

Lord, give me discernment to recognize the enemy's schemes. Open my eyes to the truth of Your Word. Help me stand firm in faith and not be swayed by fear. Let Your light expose every darkness and guide me into victory.

In Jesus' name,

Amen.

Summary Notes...

Tequeya L. Spann

CHAPTER 8

Love: What It Truly Means

"Love is patient, love is kind... it keeps no record of wrongs... Love never fails."
1 Corinthians 13:4–8 (KJV)

Love is one of the most powerful words in existence but it's also one of the most misunderstood. Too many people say "I love you" without understanding the responsibility that comes with it.

Love isn't just an emotion; it's a commitment, a choice, and an action. Real love does not hurt. Real love does not tear you down. If someone says they love you but constantly belittles you, uses you, or makes you feel small; that is not love. That's manipulation.

Love builds you up, it brings peace, and it reflects the heart of God. Many women have been made to believe that love means enduring pain just to say they have someone. But love is not meant to break you. It is meant to bless you.

Before you can truly love someone else, you must first love yourself and know who you are in Christ. When you love from a place of wholeness, not desperation, you attract the kind of love that honors you.

God's Word teaches that love is patient and kind. Love does not envy or boast. It does not dishonor others or keep a record of wrongs.

If love feels like bondage, it's not from God. God's love is freeing—it allows you to grow and still be yourself.

Poem *"You Said You Love Me"*

He said he loved me…
But he belittled me,
Called me out my name.
He said he loved me,
But his hands caused pain—
And I told myself, "Maybe I provoked him."
He said he loved me,
But he cheated,

With my friend, my family.
He said he loved me,
But he stopped coming home,
Stopped calling,
Stopped caring.
He said he loved me,
But I was only a convenience.
He said he loved me,
But love doesn't look like this.

A Moment of Reflection

• Have I mistaken attention for love?

• Am I loving from wholeness, or from a place of emptiness?

• How can I let God's love teach me how to love others better?

Closing Prayer

Lord, teach me what real love looks like. Help me to love others without losing myself. Remove every counterfeit connection that doesn't serve my soul. Fill me with Your perfect love that casts out fear so I can walk in peace and give love freely.

Amen.

Summary Notes...

Tequeya L. Spann

CHAPTER 9

Strength: Standing Firm Through the Storms

"God is our refuge and strength, a very present help in trouble."
Psalm 46:1 (KJV)

Life will test you in ways you never expected. Sometimes it feels like everything you've worked for is falling apart, like the very ground beneath you is shaking. But it's in those moments that God is strengthening your foundation.

When storms come, it's easy to ask, "Why me?" But strength is not built in calm waters—it's forged in the waves. Every trial teaches endurance, every setback builds resilience, and every tear waters the seeds of purpose inside you.

I've learned that strength isn't about pretending everything is fine. It's about showing up even when your heart is heavy. It's about saying, "God, I don't understand, but I still trust You." True strength is surrender—it's letting go of control and allowing God to fight your battles. You can't always stop the storm, but you can choose how you stand in it. When you keep your eyes on God, He'll give you peace that doesn't make sense. The winds may blow, but they won't break you, because you're rooted in His Word.

People may walk away, but God remains. Circumstances may change, but His promises do not. You've made it through things that should have destroyed you, because His strength carried you when yours ran out.

A Moment of Reflection

• What storm have you survived that showed you God's power?

• Are there areas in your life where you've been

relying on your own strength instead of His?

- How can you remind yourself of God's faithfulness during trials?

Closing Prayer

Lord, thank You for being my strength when I am weak. Remind me that storms don't come to destroy me, they come to develop me. Give me courage to stand firm in faith, even when life feels uncertain. Help me to trust that Your power is made perfect in my weakness.

Amen.

Summary Notes...

Tequeya L. Spann

CHAPTER 10

Renewal: Rededicating Your Life to Christ

"Therefore if any man be in Christ, he is a new creature: old things are passed away; behold, all things are become new."
2 Corinthians 5:17 (KJV)

At some point, each of us reaches a crossroads—where we realize that all the running, searching, and striving won't fill the empty space inside. That's when God whispers, "Come home."

Renewal begins when you stop trying to fix yourself and start surrendering yourself. You can't truly change until you allow God to take control. You've tried it your way long enough—now it's time to let Him lead.

There's a peace that comes when you finally decide to walk with Jesus. It doesn't mean life becomes perfect; it means you no longer walk alone. You start seeing your past not as a chain, but as a testimony. Everything you went through was preparation for where God is taking you.

When you rededicate your life to Christ, you are declaring that the old you no longer has power. The habits, the hurts, the shame of it defines you anymore.

You are made new. You are forgiven. You are loved. Some people may not understand your transformation. They'll question your motives or remind you of who you used to be. But let them talk. God is doing a new thing in you, and their opinions can't stop His plan.

Renewal is about release. It's about laying down your will and picking up His Word. It's realizing that every day is another chance to live with purpose and joy. You're not too far gone. You're not too broken. God still has work for you to do.

A Moment of Reflection

• What areas of my life do I need to surrender to God today?

• Am I ready to walk in the newness of life that Christ offers?

• What does a renewed relationship with Jesus look like for me?

Closing Prayer (A Prayer of Rededication)

Heavenly Father,

Thank You for never giving up on me. Thank You for loving me through my flaws, my failures, and my fears. Today, I rededicate my life to You. Wash me clean from the inside out and make me whole again. Fill me with Your Spirit so that I may live in obedience to Your will. Guide my steps, guard my heart, and use my life to glorify You. From this day forward, I am Yours.

In Jesus' name,

Amen.

Summary Notes...

Tequeya L. Spann

EPILOGUE

Waking Up My Purpose

At one point, I felt like it took me forever to write this book. But I've come to realize, it happened at the right time. God never moves too fast or too slow; He moves in His perfect timing.

This book is more than words on a page. It's a testimony, a warning, and an invitation. It's about exposing the schemes of the enemy and reminding you that no matter how far you've fallen, God's grace can still reach you.

We are living in times where distractions are everywhere. The enemy is busy, trying to steal our peace, our focus, and our purpose. But God is calling us to wake up, to see with spiritual eyes, to stand firm in faith, and to live with divine intention.

You don't have to be perfect to be chosen. You

just have to be willing. The Lord takes broken pieces and makes something beautiful. You are not behind. You are not forgotten. You are being prepared. Now is the time to walk boldly in who God called you to be.

Now is the time to wake up your purpose.

Final Prayer

Bringing Souls Back to Christ

Heavenly Father,

Thank You for every reader of this book. Thank You for every heart that felt broken, every soul that felt forgotten. Lord, I ask that You draw them closer to You. If they don't know You yet, reveal Yourself to them through Your love and mercy. If they've strayed away, call them home with open arms.

Jesus, You are our redeemer, our healer, our Savior. Help us to see ourselves through Your eyes. Help us to forgive, to heal, and to stand strong in faith. Let this book be more than words—let it be a vessel of transformation. For those who feel lost, remind them that they can always start again. For those who feel weary, renew their strength. And for those who are ready to walk in purpose—equip them, guide them, and cover them in Your grace.

In Jesus' name,

Amen.

About the Author

Tequeya Spann is the founder of Walking With a Purpose, a faith-based organization devoted to empowering women to rise above life's challenges through mentorship, spiritual growth, and community support. Born and raised in Gary, Indiana, Tequeya has devoted her life to helping others find purpose, healing, and strength through Christ.

She is a devoted mother of six children and a proud grandmother of two whom she loves deeply. Her compassion also extends to the many children she has cared for through childcare. Each one is a part of her extended family; and to the precious little ones she has adopted in love.

Her heart for nurturing others reflects the very essence of her mission: to guide with grace, patience, and unconditional love. Tequeya credits her courage and perseverance to her mother, Jacquelyn Davis, whose steadfast faith and support have always stood as a foundation in her life.

Through her writing, teaching, and outreach, Tequeya continues to uplift women and families everywhere, helping them to rediscover their worth, strengthen their faith, and walk boldly in their God-given purpose.

Tequeya L. Spann

www.ingramcontent.com/pod-product-compliance
Lightning Source LLC
LaVergne TN
LVHW010942110826
845149LV00013B/2726

* 9 7 9 8 9 9 5 1 8 2 1 0 8 *